Selections From

Cameron Mackintosh Presents
Boublil and Schönberg's

Les Misérables

™

A Musical by
Alain Boublil & Claude-Michel Schönberg

Lyrics by Herbert Kretzmer

based on the novel by VICTOR HUGO

Music by CLAUDE-MICHEL SCHÖNBERG
Lyrics by HERBERT KRETZMER
Original French text by ALAIN BOUBLIL
and JEAN-MARC NATEL
Additional material by JAMES FENTON

Orchestral score by JOHN CAMERON
Production Musical Supervisor ROBERT BILLIG
Musical Director JAMES MAY
Sound by ANDREW BRUCE/AUTOGRAPH

Associate Director and Executive Producer
RICHARD JAY-ALEXANDER
Executive Producer MARTIN McCALLUM
Casting by JOHNSON-LIFF & ZERMAN
General Management ALAN WASSER

Designed by JOHN NAPIER
Lighting by DAVID HERSEY
Costumes by ANDREANE NEOFITOU

Directed and Adapted by
TREVOR NUNN & JOHN CAIRD

THE MUSICAL SENSATION
1987 TONY® AWARD BEST MUSICAL

CON...

ISBN 978-0-7935-4893-4

This edition Copyright © 1995 by Alain Boublil Music Ltd. (ASCAP)
c/o Spielman Koenigsberg & Parker, LLP
1675 Broadway, 20th Floor, New York, New York 10019
Tel: (212) 453-2500 Fax: (212) 453-2550 e-mail: ABML@skpny.co
All songs sub-published for the UK and Eire by Alain Boublil (Overseas) Ltd. (PRS), 9 Collingham Gardens, London, England SW5 0HS

ALAIN BOUBLIL MUSIC LTD.

EXCLUSIVELY DISTRIBUTED BY

7777 W. BLUEMOUND RD. P.O. BOX 13819 MILWAUKEE, WI 53213

Visit Hal Leonard Online at
www.halleonard.com

AT THE END OF THE DAY

Flute

Music by CLAUDE-MICHEL SCHÖNBERG
Lyrics by ALAIN BOUBLIL, JEAN-MARC NATEL
and HERBERT KRETZMER

BRING HIM HOME

Flute

Music by CLAUDE-MICHEL SCHÖNBERG
Lyrics by HERBERT KRETZMER and ALAIN BOUBLIL

CASTLE ON A CLOUD

Flute

Music by CLAUDE-MICHEL SCHÖNBERG
Lyrics by ALAIN BOUBLIL, JEAN-MARC NATEL
and HERBERT KRETZMER

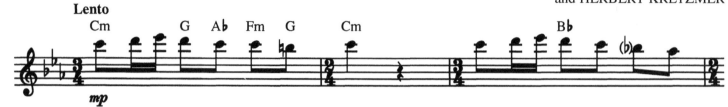

DO YOU HEAR THE PEOPLE SING?

Flute

Music by CLAUDE-MICHEL SCHÖNBERG
Lyrics by ALAIN BOUBLIL, JEAN-MARC NATEL
and HERBERT KRETZMER

DRINK WITH ME
(To Days Gone By)

Flute

Music by CLAUDE-MICHEL SCHÖNBERG
Lyrics by ALAIN BOUBLIL and HERBERT KRETZMER

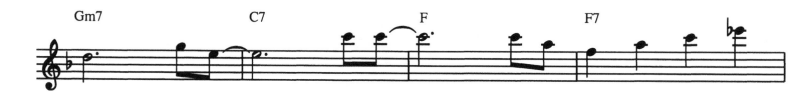

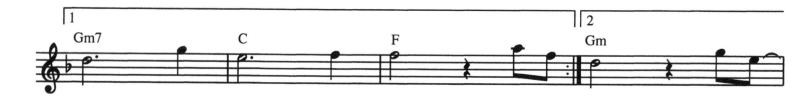

EMPTY CHAIRS AT EMPTY TABLES

Flute

Music by CLAUDE-MICHEL SCHÖNBERG
Lyrics by ALAIN BOUBLIL and HERBERT KRETZMER

A HEART FULL OF LOVE

Flute

Music by CLAUDE-MICHEL SCHÖNBERG
Lyrics by ALAIN BOUBLIL, JEAN-MARC NATEL
and HERBERT KRETZMER

I DREAMED A DREAM

Flute

Music by CLAUDE-MICHEL SCHÖNBERG
Lyrics by ALAIN BOUBLIL, JEAN-MARC NATEL
and HERBERT KRETZMER

IN MY LIFE

Flute

Music by CLAUDE-MICHEL SCHÖNBERG
Lyrics by ALAIN BOUBLIL, JEAN-MARC NATEL
and HERBERT KRETZMER

A LITTLE FALL OF RAIN

Flute

Music by CLAUDE-MICHEL SCHÖNBERG
Lyrics by ALAIN BOUBLIL, JEAN-MARC NATEL
and HERBERT KRETZMER

ON MY OWN

Music by CLAUDE-MICHEL SCHÖNBERG
Lyrics by ALAIN BOUBLIL, JEAN-MARC NATEL,
HERBERT KRETZMER, JOHN CAIRD and TREVOR NUNN

Flute

STARS

Flute

Music by CLAUDE-MICHEL SCHÖNBERG
Lyrics by HERBERT KRETZMER and ALAIN BOUBLIL

WHO AM I?

Music by CLAUDE-MICHEL SCHÖNBERG
Lyrics by ALAIN BOUBLIL, JEAN-MARC NATEL
and HERBERT KRETZMER

Flute

HAL·LEONARD INSTRUMENTAL PLAY-ALONG

Your favorite songs are arranged just for solo instrumentalists with this outstanding series. Each book includes great full-accompaniment play-along audio so you can sound just like a pro! Check out **www.halleonard.com** to see all the titles available.

The Beatles

All You Need Is Love • Blackbird • Day Tripper • Eleanor Rigby • Get Back • Here, There and Everywhere • Hey Jude • I Will • Let It Be • Lucy in the Sky with Diamonds • Ob-La-Di, Ob-La-Da • Penny Lane • Something • Ticket to Ride • Yesterday.

_____ 00225330	Flute	$14.99
_____ 00225331	Clarinet	$14.99
_____ 00225332	Alto Sax	$14.99
_____ 00225333	Tenor Sax	$14.99
_____ 00225334	Trumpet	$14.99
_____ 00225335	Horn	$14.99
_____ 00225336	Trombone	$14.99
_____ 00225337	Violin	$14.99
_____ 00225338	Viola	$14.99
_____ 00225339	Cello	$14.99

Chart Hits

All About That Bass • All of Me • Happy • Radioactive • Roar • Say Something • Shake It Off • A Sky Full of Stars • Someone like You • Stay with Me • Thinking Out Loud • Uptown Funk.

_____ 00146207	Flute	$12.99
_____ 00146208	Clarinet	$12.99
_____ 00146209	Alto Sax	$12.99
_____ 00146210	Tenor Sax	$12.99
_____ 00146211	Trumpet	$12.99
_____ 00146212	Horn	$12.99
_____ 00146213	Trombone	$12.99
_____ 00146214	Violin	$12.99
_____ 00146215	Viola	$12.99
_____ 00146216	Cello	$12.99

Disney Greats

Arabian Nights • Hawaiian Roller Coaster Ride • It's a Small World • Look Through My Eyes • Yo Ho (A Pirate's Life for Me) • and more.

_____ 00841934	Flute	$12.99
_____ 00841935	Clarinet	$12.99
_____ 00841936	Alto Sax	$12.99
_____ 00841937	Tenor Sax	$12.95
_____ 00841938	Trumpet	$12.99
_____ 00841939	Horn	$12.99
_____ 00841940	Trombone	$12.99
_____ 00841941	Violin	$12.99
_____ 00841942	Viola	$12.99
_____ 00841943	Cello	$12.99
_____ 00842078	Oboe	$12.99

The Greatest Showman

Come Alive • From Now On • The Greatest Show • A Million Dreams • Never Enough • The Other Side • Rewrite the Stars • This Is Me • Tightrope.

_____ 00277389	Flute	$14.99
_____ 00277390	Clarinet	$14.99
_____ 00277391	Alto Sax	$14.99
_____ 00277392	Tenor Sax	$14.99
_____ 00277393	Trumpet	$14.99
_____ 00277394	Horn	$14.99
_____ 00277395	Trombone	$14.99
_____ 00277396	Violin	$14.99
_____ 00277397	Viola	$14.99
_____ 00277398	Cello	$14.99

Movie and TV Music

The Avengers • Doctor Who XI • Downton Abbey • Game of Thrones • Guardians of the Galaxy • Hawaii Five-O • Married Life • Rey's Theme (from *Star Wars: The Force Awakens*) • The X-Files • and more.

_____ 00261807	Flute	$12.99
_____ 00261808	Clarinet	$12.99
_____ 00261809	Alto Sax	$12.99
_____ 00261810	Tenor Sax	$12.99
_____ 00261811	Trumpet	$12.99
_____ 00261812	Horn	$12.99
_____ 00261813	Trombone	$12.99
_____ 00261814	Violin	$12.99
_____ 00261815	Viola	$12.99
_____ 00261816	Cello	$12.99

12 Pop Hits

Believer • Can't Stop the Feeling • Despacito • It Ain't Me • Look What You Made Me Do • Million Reasons • Perfect • Send My Love (To Your New Lover) • Shape of You • Slow Hands • Too Good at Goodbyes • What About Us.

_____ 00261790	Flute	$12.99
_____ 00261791	Clarinet	$12.99
_____ 00261792	Alto Sax	$12.99
_____ 00261793	Tenor Sax	$12.99
_____ 00261794	Trumpet	$12.99
_____ 00261795	Horn	$12.99
_____ 00261796	Trombone	$12.99
_____ 00261797	Violin	$12.99
_____ 00261798	Viola	$12.99
_____ 00261799	Cello	$12.99

Songs from Frozen, Tangled and Enchanted

Do You Want to Build a Snowman? • For the First Time in Forever • Happy Working Song • I See the Light • In Summer • Let It Go • Mother Knows Best • That's How You Know • True Love's First Kiss • When Will My Life Begin • and more.

_____ 00126921	Flute	$14.99
_____ 00126922	Clarinet	$14.99
_____ 00126923	Alto Sax	$14.99
_____ 00126924	Tenor Sax	$14.99
_____ 00126925	Trumpet	$14.99
_____ 00126926	Horn	$14.99
_____ 00126927	Trombone	$14.99
_____ 00126928	Violin	$14.99
_____ 00126929	Viola	$14.99
_____ 00126930	Cello	$14.99

Top Hits

Adventure of a Lifetime • Budapest • Die a Happy Man • Ex's & Oh's • Fight Song • Hello • Let It Go • Love Yourself • One Call Away • Pillowtalk • Stitches • Writing's on the Wall.

_____ 00171073	Flute	$12.99
_____ 00171074	Clarinet	$12.99
_____ 00171075	Alto Sax	$12.99
_____ 00171106	Tenor Sax	$12.99
_____ 00171107	Trumpet	$12.99
_____ 00171108	Horn	$12.99
_____ 00171109	Trombone	$12.99
_____ 00171110	Violin	$12.99
_____ 00171111	Viola	$12.99
_____ 00171112	Cello	$12.99

Wicked

As Long As You're Mine • Dancing Through Life • Defying Gravity • For Good • I'm Not That Girl • Popular • The Wizard and I • and more.

_____ 00842236	Flute	$12.99
_____ 00842237	Clarinet	$12.99
_____ 00842238	Alto Saxophone	$12.99
_____ 00842239	Tenor Saxophone	$11.95
_____ 00842240	Trumpet	$12.99
_____ 00842241	Horn	$12.99
_____ 00842242	Trombone	$12.99
_____ 00842243	Violin	$12.99
_____ 00842244	Viola	$12.99
_____ 00842245	Cello	$12.99

HAL·LEONARD®